AF095764

# CELEBRATING THE FAMILY NAME OF WILSON

# Celebrating the Family Name of Wilson

Walter the Educator

Silent King Books
a WhichHead Entertainment Imprint

Copyright © 2024 by Walter the Educator

All rights reserved. No part of this book may be reproduced in any manner whatsoever without written permission except in the case of brief quotations embodied in critical articles and reviews.

First Printing, 2024

Disclaimer

This book is a literary work; the story is not about specific persons, locations, situations, and/or circumstances unless mentioned in a historical context. Any resemblance to real persons, locations, situations, and/or circumstances is coincidental. This book is for entertainment and informational purposes only. The author and publisher offer this information without warranties expressed or implied. No matter the grounds, neither the author nor the publisher will be accountable for any losses, injuries, or other damages caused by the reader's use of this book. The use of this book acknowledges an understanding and acceptance of this disclaimer.

Celebrating the Family Name of Wilson is a memory book that belongs to the Celebrating Family Name Book Series by Walter the Educator. Collect them all and more books at WaltertheEducator.com

**USE THE EXTRA SPACE TO DOCUMENT YOUR FAMILY MEMORIES THROUGHOUT THE YEARS**

# WILSON

In the heart of hills, where echoes dance,
Celebrating the Family Name of

# Wilson

And rivers sing a timeless song,

There rises a name, a sacred trance—

Wilson, strong and everlong.

Through rugged winds and quiet dawns,

In fields where ancient trees still grow,

The Wilson name, like oak and stone,

Has weathered storms, withstood the snow.

A lineage deep as ocean's breath,

Each wave a tale of grit and grace,

From whispered dreams to roaring quests,

The Wilsons carved their destined place.

In every hand, a tale is spun,

Of courage bold and kindness rare,

From fathers, sons, to daughters, mums,

Their legacy beyond compare.
## Celebrating the Family Name of

# Wilson

The forge of time, it molds their steel,

In fires of love and lands afar,

With every spark, a truth revealed—

A Wilson's heart, a guiding star.

They walk the path where shadows dwell,

Yet light the way for those who follow,

With wisdom old and stories swell,

Each Wilson voice a steady bellow.

In homes where laughter fills the air,

And hearths are warm with joy and song,

The Wilsons gather, strong and fair,

To celebrate the ties lifelong.

Their roots are deep in earthen clay,

Yet branches reach the sky's embrace,

In every Wilson, bright as day,
Celebrating the Family Name of

# Wilson

The future's hope, a shining face.

Through seasons' change and trials faced,

Their bond remains unbreakable,

.

With every step, a mark is traced—

A legacy unshakable.

From ancient clans with swords in hand,

To modern minds with dreams so wide,

The Wilson spirit, proud and grand,
Celebrating the Family Name of

# Wilson

Has crossed the seas, has touched the sky.

# ABOUT THE CREATOR

Walter the Educator is one of the pseudonyms for Walter Anderson. Formally educated in Chemistry, Business, and Education, he is an educator, an author, a diverse entrepreneur, and he is the son of a disabled war veteran. "Walter the Educator" shares his time between educating and creating. He holds interests and owns several creative projects that entertain, enlighten, enhance, and educate, hoping to inspire and motivate you. Follow, find new works, and stay up to date with Walter the Educator™

at WaltertheEducator.com

www.ingramcontent.com/pod-product-compliance
Lightning Source LLC
LaVergne TN
LVHW052009060526
838201LV00059B/3928